Dedication
To all those who ever struggled with learning a foreign language and to Wolfgang Karfunkel

Also by Yatir Nitzany

Conversational Spanish Quick and Easy

Conversational French Quick and Easy

Conversational Italian Quick and Easy

Conversational Portuguese Quick and Easy

Conversational German Quick and Easy

Conversational Dutch Quick and Easy

Conversational Norwegian Quick and Easy

Conversational Danish Quick and Easy

Conversational Russian Quick and Easy

Conversational Ukrainian Quick and Easy

Conversational Bulgarian Quick and Easy

Conversational Polish Quick and Easy

Conversational Hebrew Quick and Easy

Conversational Yiddish Quick and Easy

Conversational Armenian Quick and Easy

Conversational Arabic Quick and Easy

Conversational French Quick and Easy
The Most Innovative Technique to Learn the French Language

Part II

YATIR NITZANY

Translated by:
Semadar Mercedes Friedman

Interior Design:
Menachem Otto

Copyright © 2019
Yatir Nitzany
All rights reserved.
ISBN: 978-1951244446
Printed in the United States of America

Foreword

About Myself

For many years I struggled to learn Spanish, and I still knew no more than about twenty words. Consequently, I was extremely frustrated. One day I stumbled upon this method as I was playing around with word combinations. Suddenly, I came to the realization that every language has a certain core group of words that are most commonly used and, simply by learning them, one could gain the ability to engage in quick and easy conversational Spanish.

I discovered which words those were, and I narrowed them down to three hundred and fifty that, once memorized, one could connect and create one's own sentences. The variations were and are *infinite*! By using this incredibly simple technique, I could converse at a proficient level and speak Spanish. Within a week, I astonished my Spanish-speaking friends with my newfound ability. The next semester I registered at my university for a Spanish language course, and I applied the same principles I had learned in that class (grammar, additional vocabulary, future and past tense, etc.) to those three hundred and fifty words I already had memorized, and immediately I felt as if I had grown wings and learned how to fly.

At the end of the semester, we took a class trip to San José, Costa Rica. I was like a fish in water, while the rest of my classmates were floundering and still struggling to converse. Throughout the following months, I again applied the same principle to other languages—French, Portuguese, Italian, and Arabic, all of which I now speak proficiently, thanks to this very simple technique.

This method is by far the fastest way to master quick and easy conversational language skills. There is no other technique that compares to my concept. It is effective, it worked for me, and it will work for you. Be consistent with my program, and you too will succeed the way I and many, many others have.

Table of Contents

Introduction to the Program 9

Introduction to the French Language 11

Memorization Made Easy 12

The Program
- Travel 15
- Transportation 19
- City 21
- Entertainment 25
- Foods 29
- Vegetables 33
- Fruits 35
- Shopping 37
- Family 41
- Human Body 43
- Health 45
- Emergencies and Natural Disasters 49
- Home 53

Basic Grammatical Requirements of the French Language 57

French Pronunciation 58

Conclusion 59

Note from the Author 60

Introduction to the Program

In the first book, you were taught the 350 most useful words in the French language, which, once memorized, could be combined in order for you to create your own sentences. Now, with the knowledge you have gained, you can use those words in Conversational French Quick and Easy Part 2 and Part 3, in order to supplement the 350 words that you've already memorized. This combination of words and sentences will help you master the language to even greater proficiency and quicker than with other courses.

The books that comprise Parts 2 and 3 have progressed from just vocabulary and are now split into various categories that are useful in our everyday lives. These categories range from travel to food to school and work, and other similarly broad subjects. In contrast to various other methods, the topics that are covered also contain parts of vocabulary that are not often broached, such as the military, politics, and religion. With these more unusual topics for learning conversational languages, the student can learn quicker and easier. This method is flawless and it has proven itself time and time again.

If you decide to travel to France, then this book will help you speak the French language.

This method has worked for me and thousands of others. It surpasses any other language-learning method system currently on the market today.

This book, Part 2, specifically deals with practical aspects concerning travel, camping, transportation, city living, entertainment such as films, food including vegetables and fruit, shopping, family including grandparents, in-laws, and stepchildren, human anatomy, health, emergencies, and natural disasters, and home situations.

The sentences within each category can help you get by in other countries.

In relation to travel, for example, you are given sentences about food, airport necessities such as immigration, and passports. Helpful phrases include, "Where is the immigration and passport control inside the airport?" and "I want to order a bowl of cereal and toast with jelly." For flights there are informative combinations such as, "There is a long line of passengers in the terminal because of the delay on the runway." When arriving in another country options for what to say include, "We want to hire a driver for the tour. However, we want to pay with a credit card instead of cash" and, "On which street is the car-rental agency?"

When discussing entertainment in another country and in a new language, you are provided with sentences and vocabulary that will help you interact with others. You can discuss art galleries and watching foreign films. For example, you may need to say to friends, "I need subtitles if I watch a foreign film" and, 'The mystery-suspense genre films are usually good movies'. You can talk about your own filming experience in front of the camera.

The selection of topics in this book is much wider than in ordinary courses. By including social issue such as incarceration, it will help you to engage with more people who speak the language you are learning.

Part 3 will deal with vocabulary and sentences relevant to indoor matters such as school and the office, but also a variety of professions and sports.

The French Language

The French language originated in France. It is a Romance language as are Spanish, Portuguese, Italian, and Romanian since they all descend from what originally was the spoken Latin language. In the sixteenth century, King Francis I declared French as his nation's official language. Little did he know it was soon to become the fifteenth most-common language in the world and the official language of almost thirty countries.

The French language was once used in diplomatic circles and was also a symbol of prestige, meaning only the nobility and higher classes of educated people spoke it. Russia's Catherine the Great and all her court communicated in French, as well as Prussia's Frederick II. Today, because of France's colonial expansion between the seventeenth and twentieth centuries, there are now twenty-nine countries where French is the official language. Despite its many dialects French is still spoken in all its former colonies. However, the language has declined in popularity since its peak in the sixteen and seventeenth centuries. But French is again rising in popularity. It has sixteen million students and 220 million native speakers.

Memorization Made Easy

There is no doubt the three hundred and fifty words in my program are the required essentials in order to engage in quick and easy basic conversation in any foreign language. However, some people may experience difficulty in the memorization. For this reason, I created Memorization Made Easy. This memorization technique will make this program so simple and fun that it's unbelievable! I have spread the words over the following twenty pages. Each page contains a vocabulary table of ten to fifteen words. Below every vocabulary box, sentences are composed from the words on the page that you have just studied. This aids greatly in memorization. Once you succeed in memorizing the first page, then proceed to the second page. Upon completion of the second page, go back to the first and review. Then proceed to the third page. After memorizing the third, go back to the first and second and repeat. And so on. As you continue, begin to combine words and create your own sentences in your head. Every time you proceed to the following page, you will notice words from the previous pages will be present in those simple sentences as well, because repetition is one of the most crucial aspects in learning any foreign language. Upon completion of your twenty pages, *congratulations,* you have absorbed the required words and gained a basic, quick-and-easy proficiency and you should now be able to create your own sentences and say anything you wish in the French language. This is a crash course in conversational French, and it works!

The Program *"Conversational French Quick and Easy"* Let's Begin!

TRAVEL - LE VOYAGE

Flight - Le vol
Airplane - L'avion
Airport – L'aéroport / **Terminal** - La terminal
Passport - Le passeport / **Customs** - Les douanes
Take off (airplane) – Le décollage / **Landing** - L'atterrissage
Departure - Le départ / **Arrival** – L'arrivée
Gate - Porte
Luggage - Le bagage / **Suitcase** - La Valise
Baggage claim - Réclamation du bagages
Passenger – **(Male)** Passager / **(Female)** passagère
Final Destination – La destination finale
Boarding - L'embarquement
Runway - La piste
Line - La ligne
Delay - Le retard
Wing - L'aile

I like to travel.
J'aime voyager.
This is a very expensive flight.
C'est un très cher vol.
The airplane takes off in the morning and lands at night.
L'avion décolle le matin et atterrit la nuit.
My suitcase is at the baggage claim.
Ma valise est à la récupération des bagages.
We need to go to the departure gate instead of the arrival gate.
Nous devons aller à la porte du départ au lieu de la porte d'arrivée.
There is a long line of passengers in the terminal because of the delay on the runway.
Il y a une longue file de passagers dans le terminal à cause du retard sur la piste.
What is your final destination?
Quelle est votre destination finale?
I don't like to sit above the wing of the airplane.
Je n'aime pas m'asseoir au-dessus de l'aile de l'avion.
The flight takes off at 3pm, but the boarding commences at 2:20pm.
Le vol décolle à 15h, mais l'embarquement commence à 14h20.
Do I need to check in my luggage?
Dois-je enregistrer mes bagages?
Where is the passport control inside the airport?
Où est le contrôle des passeports se trouve dans l'aéroport
I am almost finished at customs.
J'ai presque fini aux douanes.

International flight – Vol international
Domestic flight – Vol national
First class – Première classe / **Business class** – Classe d'affaire
Economy class – Classe économique
Round trip - Aller et retour / **One-way flight** - Un vol
Return flight - Vol de retour
Direct flight - Vol direct
Flight attendant - L'hôtesse d'air / agent de bord
Layover / connection - Escale / connection
Reservation - Réservation
Security check – Vérification de sécurité
Checked bags - Sacs enregistrés / **Carry on bag** - Bagage à main
Business trip - Voyage d'affaires
Check in counter – Comptoir d'enregistrement
Travel agency - Agence de voyage
Temporary visa – Visa temporaire / **Permanent visa** – Visa permanente
Country – Pays

The flight attendant told me to go to the check in counter.
L'hôtesse de l'air m'a dit d'aller au comptoir d'enregistrement.
For international flights, you must be at the airport three hours before the flight.
Pour les vols internationaux, vous devez être à l'aéroport trois heures avant le vol.
For a domestic flight, I need to arrive at the airport at least two hours before the flight.
Pour un vol intérieur, je dois arriver à l'aéroport au moins deux heures avant le vol.
Business class is usually cheaper than first class.
La classe affaires est généralement moins chère que la première classe.
I purchased my plane tickets at the travel agency.
J'achète mon billet d'avion chez l'agence des voyages.
The one-way ticket is cheaper than the round-trip ticket.
Le billet de un vol est moins cher que le billet aller-retour.
I prefer a direct flight without a layover.
Je préfère un vol direct sans escale.
I must make reservations for my return flight.
Je dois faire des réservations pour mon vol de retour.
Why do I need to remove my shoes at the security check?
Pourquoi dois-je retirer mes chaussures lors du contrôle de sécurité?
I have three checked bags and one carry-on.
J'ai trois bagages enregistrés et un valise ala main.
I have to ask my travel agent if this country requires an entry visa.
Je dois demander à mon agent de voyage si ce pays a exige un visa d'entrée.
I have to ask my travel agent if this country requires a visa.
Je dois demander à mon agent de voyage si ce pays a besoin d'un visa.

Travel

Trip – Voyage
Tourist - Touriste / **Tourism** - Tourisme
Holiday - Fêtes / **Vacations** - Les vacances
Currency exchange - Échange de devises
Port of entry - Port d'entrée
Car rental agency - Agence de location de voitures
Identification - Identification
GPS - GPS
Road - Route
Map - Carte
Information center - Centre d'information
Bank - Banque
Hotel – Hôtel / **Motel** - Motel / **Hostel** - Auberge
Leisure - Loisir
Driver – **(Male)** Chauffeur / **(Female)** Chauffeuse
Tour - Tour
Credit - Crédit / **Cash** - Cash
A travel guide - Un guide de voyage
Ski resort - Station de ski

I had an amazing trip.
J'ai fait un voyage étonnant.
The currency exchange counter is past the port of entry.
Le bureau de change est en passant la porte d'entrée.
There is a lot of tourism during the holidays and vacations.
Il y a beaucoup de tourisme pendant les fêtes et les vacances.
Where is the car-rental agency?
Où est l'agence de location de voitures?
You need to show your identification whenever checking in at a hotel.
Vous devez présenter votre pièce d'identité lors de l'enregistrement dans un hôtel.
It's more convenient to use the GPS on the roads instead of a map.
Il est plus pratique d'utiliser le GPS sur les routes plutôt que une carte.
Why is the information center closed today?
Pourquoi le centre d'information est-il fermé aujourd'hui?
When I am in a new country, I go to the bank before I go to the hotel.
Quand je suis dans un nouveau pays, je vais à la banque avant d'aller à l'hôtel.
I need to book my leisure vacation at the ski resort today.
Je dois réserver mes vacances de loisirs dans la station de ski dès aujourd'hui.
We want to hire a driver for the tour.
Nous voulons embaucher un chauffeur/chauffeuse pour la visite.
We want to pay with a credit card instead of cash.
Nous voulons payer avec une carte de crédit plutôt que cash.
Does the tour include an English-speaking guide?
La visite comprend-elle un guide anglophone?

TRANSPORTATION - TRANSPORT

Car - Voiture
Bus - Autobus
Station - Station
Train - Train / **Train station -** Gare
Train tracks - Voies ferrées / **Train cart -** Chariot de train
Subway - Métro
Ticket - Billet
Taxi - Taxi
Motorcycle - Motociclete / **Scooter -** Scooter
Helicopter - Hélicoptère
School bus – Bus scolaire
Limousine - Limousine
Driver license - Permis de conduire
Vehicle registration - Immatriculation des véhicules
License plate - Plaque d'immatriculation
Ticket (penalty) - Amende / contravention

Where is the public transportation?
Où sont les transports public?
Where can I buy a bus ticket?
Où puis-je acheter un ticket de bus?
Please call a taxi.
S'il vous plaît appeler un taxi.
In some cities, you don't need a car because you can rely on the subway.
Dans certaines villes, vous n'avez pas besoin de voiture car vous pouvez compter sur le métro.
Where is the train station?
Où est la gare?
The train cart is still stuck on the tracks.
Le chariot de train est encore coincé sur les voies.
The motorcycles make loud noises.
Les motos font des bruits forts.
Where can I rent a scooter?
Où puis-je louer un scooter?
I want to schedule a helicopter tour.
Je veux planifier un tour en hélicoptère.
I want to go to the party in a limousine.
Je veux aller à la fête en limousine.
Don't forget to bring your driver's license and registration.
N'oubliez pas d'apporter votre permis de conduire et votre inscription.
The cop gave me a ticket because my license plate is expired.
L'agent de police m'a donné une amende parce que ma plaque d'immatriculation a expirée.

Truck – Un camion
Pickup truck - Camionnette
Bicycle – Vélo
Van - Vann
Gas station – Station-d'essence
Gasoline - De l'essence
Tire - Pneu
Oil change – Changement d'huile
Tire change – Changement de pneu
Mechanic – Mécanicien
Canoe - Canoë
Ship - Navire / **Boat** – Bateau
Yacht - Yacht
Sailboat - Voilier / **Motorboat** - Bateau à moteur
Marina - Marinna / **A dock** - Le quai
Cruise - Croisière / **Cruise ship** - Bateau de croisière
Ferry - Ferry
Submarine - Sous-marin

I can put my bicycle in my truck.
Je peux mettre mon vélo dans mon camion.
Where is the gas station?
Où est la station d'essence?
I need gasoline and also to put air in my tires.
J'ai besoin d'essence et aussi de mettre de l'air dans mes pneus.
I need to take my car to the mechanic for a tire and oil change.
Je dois amener ma voiture chez le mécanicien pour un changement de pneu et d'huile.
I can put my canoe in the van.
Je peux apporter mon canoë dans la camionnette.
Can I bring my yacht to the boat show at the marina?
Puis-je amener mon yacht au salon nautique de la marina?
I prefer a motorboat instead of a sailboat.
Je préfère un bateau à moteur au lieu d'un voilier.
I want to leave my boat at the dock on the island.
Je veux laisser mon bateau sur le quai de l'île.
This spot is a popular stopping point for the cruise ship.
Cet endroit est un point d'arrêt populaire pour le bateau de croisière.
This was an incredible cruise.
Ce fut une croisière incroyable.
Do you have the schedule for the ferry?
Avez-vous l'horaire du ferry?
The submarine is yellow.
Le sous-marin est jaune.

CITY - VILLE

Village - Village
House - Maison / **Home -** Foyer
Apartment - Appartement
Tower - La tour
Building - Bâtiment
Skyscraper – Gratte-ciel
Neighborhood – Quartier
Office building – Immeuble de bureaux
Post office – Bureau de poste
Location - Une location
Elevator – Ascenseur
Stairs - Escaliers
Fence - Clôture
Construction site – Chantier de construction
Bridge - Pont
Gate - Porte
City hall – Mairie
The mayor - Le maire
Fire department – Service d'incendie / **Fireman -** Les pompiers

Is this a city or a village?
Est-ce une ville ou un village?
Does he live in a house or an apartment?
Vit-il dans une maison ou un appartement?
This residential building does not have an elevator, just stairs.
Cet immeuble résidentiel n'a pas d'ascenseur, que des escaliers.
These skyscrapers are located in the new part of the city.
Ces grattes-ciel sont situés dans la nouvelle part de la ville.
The tower is tall but the building beside it is very short.
La tour est haute mais le bâtiment à côté est très bas.
This is a historical neighborhood.
Ceci est un quartier historique.
There is a fence around the construction site.
Il y a une clôture autour du chantier de construction.
The post office is located in that office building.
Le bureau de poste est situé dans cet immeuble de bureaux.
The bridge is closed today.
Le pont est fermé aujourd'hui.
The gate is open.
Le portail est ouvert.
The fire department is located in the building next to city hall.
Le service d'incendie est situé dans le bâtiment à côté de la mairie.

Street - Rue / **Main street** - Rue principale
Parking - Stationnement / **Parking lot** - Terrain de stationnement / **To Park** - Se garer
Sidewalk - Trottoir
Traffic - Circulation
Traffic light - Feu de circulation
Red light - Feu rouge / **Yellow light** - Feu jaune / **Green light** - Feu vert
Toll lane - Voie de péage
Fast lane - Voie rapide / **Slow lane** - Voie lente
Left lane - Voie gauche / **Right lane** - File de droite
Highway - Autoroute / **Intersection** - Intersection / **Tunnel** - Tunnel
To drive - Conduire
U-turn - Demi-tour / **Shortcut** - Raccouri
Stop sign - Panneau stop / **Pedestrians** - Piétons / **Crosswalk** - Passage clouté

Parking is on the main street and not on the sidewalk.
Le stationnement est sur la rue principale et pas sur le trottoir.
Where is the parking lot?
Où est le terrain de stationnement?
The traffic is very bad today.
Le trafic est très mauvais aujourd'hui.
You must avoid the fast lane because it's a toll lane.
Vous devez éviter la voie rapide car c'est une voie à péage.
I don't like to drive on the highway.
Je n'aime pas conduire sur l'autoroute.
At a red light you need to stop, at a yellow light you must be prepared to stop and at a green you can drive.
À un feu rouge, vous devez vous arrêter, à un feu jaune, vous devez être prêt à vous arrêter et à un vert, vous pouvez conduire.
This road has too many traffic lights.
Cette route a beacoup des feux de circulation
At the intersection, you need to stay in the right lane instead of the left lane because that's a bus lane.
À l'intersection, vous devez rester dans la voie droite au au lieu de la gauche car il s'agit d'une voie réservée aux bus.
The tunnel seems longer than yesterday.
Le tunnel pareil être plus long qu' hier.
This is a short drive.
Ce voyage esttrès court.
The next bus stop is far away.
Le prochain arrêt du bus est très loin.
You need to turn right at the stop sign and then continue on straight.
Vous devez tourner à droite au stop et continuer tout droit.
Pedestrians use the crosswalk to cross the road.
Les piétons utilisent le passage pour piétons pour traverser la route.

City

Capital – Capitale
Resort - Resort
Port - Port
Road - Route
Trail – Piste
Bus station - Gare de bus / station de bus
Bus stop – Arrêt de bus
Night club – Boîte de nuit
Downtown – Centre ville
District - Arrondissement / quartier
County - Comté
Statue - Statue
Monument - Monument
Castle – Château
Cathedral - Cathédrale
Zoo – Zoo
Science museum – Musée des sciences
Playground – Terrain de jeux
Swimming pool – Piscine
Jail / prison – Prison

The capital is a major attraction point for tourists.
La capitale est un point majeur d'attraction pour les touristes.
The resort is next to the port.
Le resort est à côté du port.
The night club is located in the downtown district.
La boîte de nuit est située dans le quartier du centre-ville.
This statue is a city monument.
La statue est un monument de la ville.
This is an ancient castle.
Ceci est un ancien château.
That is a beautiful cathedral.
C'est une belle cathédrale.
Do you want to go to the zoo or the science museum?
Voulez-vous aller au zoo ou au musée des sciences?
The children are in the playground.
Les enfants sont dans le terrain des jeux.
The swimming pool is closed for the community today.
La piscine est fermée pour la communauté aujourd'hui.
You need to follow the trail alongside the main street to reach the bus station.
Vous devez suivre le sentier au long de la rue principale pour rejoindre la gare du bus.
The jail in this county is very small.
La prison dans cet comté est très petite.

ENTERTAINMENT - DIVERTISSEMENT

Movie - Le film
Theater (movie theater) - Cinéma
Actor - Acteur
Actress - Actrice
Genre – Genre
Subtitles – Les sous-titres
Action - Action
Foreign - Étranger
Mystery – Mystère
Suspense – La suspense
Documentary - Documentaire / **Biography -** Biographie
Drama - Drame
Comedy - Comédie
Romance - Romance
Horror – Horreur
Animation - Animation / **Cartoon –** Dessin animé
Director – **(m)** Réalisateur / **(f)** réalisatrice
Producer - **(m)** Producteur / **(f)** productrice
Audience – Audience

There are three new movies at the theater that I want to see.
Il y a trois nouveaux films au théâtre que je veux voir.
He is a really good actor.
C'est un très bon acteur.
She is an excellent actress.
C'est une excellente actrice.
That was a good action movie.
C'était un bon film d'action.
I need subtitles if I watch a foreign film.
J'ai besoin de sous-titres si je regarde un film étranger.
Films of the mystery-suspense genre are usually good movies.
Les films du genre mystère-suspense sont généralement des bons films.
I like documentary films. However, comedy-drama or romance films are better.
J'aime les films documentaires. Mais, les films dramatiques ou romantiques sont meilleurs.
Sometimes biographies are boring to watch.
Des fois les biographies sont ennuyeuses à regarder.
My favorite genre of movies are the horror movies.
Mon genre préféré de films sont les films d'horreur.
It's fun to watch animated movies.
C'est amusant de regarder des films d'animation.
The director and the producer can meet the audience today.
Le réalisateur et le producteur peuvent rencontrer l'audience aujourd'hui.

Entertainment - Divertissement
Television - Télévision / téléviseur / télé
A show (as in television) **-** Série
A show (as in live performance) **-** Spectacle
Channel – Canal
Series - Séries
Commercial - Commercial
Episode - Épisode
Anchorman - Présentateur
Anchorwoman - Présentatrice
News - Nouvelles
News station – Station de nouvelles
Screening - Projection
Live - Direct
Broadcast - Diffuser / émission
Headlines - Titres
Viewer – (m) Téléspectateur **/ (f)** Téléspectatrice
Speech – Discours
Script - Scénario
Screen - Écran
Camera - Caméra

It's already time to buy a new television.
Il est deja temps d'acheter un nouvelle téléviseur.
This was the first episode of this television show yet it was a long series.
C'était la premiere épisode de cette émission de télévision, mais c'était une longue série.
There aren't any commercials on this channel.
Il n'y a pas de publicité sur cette chaîne.
This anchorman and anchorwoman work for our local news station.
Cette présentateur et présentatrice travaille pour notre station de nouvelles locales.
They decided to screen a live broadcast on the news.
Ils ont décidé de projeter une émission en direct sur les informations.
The news station featured the headlines before the program began.
La station des nouvelles nous donne les titres des journaux avant le début du programme.
Tonight, all the details about the incident were mentioned on the news.
Ce soir, tous les détails de l'incident ont été mentionnés dans les nouvelles.
The viewers wanted to hear the presidential speech today.
Les téléspectateurs ont voulu entendre le discours présidentiel aujourd'hui.
I must read my script in front of the screen and the camera
Je dois lire mon script devant l'écran et la caméra
We want to enjoy the entertainment tonight.
Nous voulons profiter du divertissement ce soir.

Entertainment

Theater (play) – Théâtre
A musical - Pièce musical
A play - Pièce de théâtre
Theater stage – Plateau de théâtre
Audition - Audition
Performance – Représentation / spectacle
Box office - Guichet / **Ticket** – Billet
Singer – Chanteur /(f) Chanteuse / **Band** – Bande
Orchestra - Orchestre
Opera - Opéra
Music - La musique
Song - Chanson
Musical instrument – Instrument de musique
Drum - Tambour
Guitar - Guitare
Piano - Piano
Trumpet – Trompette
Violin – Violon
Flute - Flûte
Art - Art
Gallery - Galerie
Studio - Studio
Museum – Musée

It was a great musical performance.
Ce fût un grand spectacle musicale.
Can I audition for the play on this stage?
Puis-je auditionner pour la pièce sur cette scène?
She is the lead singer of the band.
Elle est la chanteuse principale du groupe.
I will go to the box office tomorrow to purchase tickets for the opera.
J'irai au guichet demain pour acheter des billets de l'opéra.
The orchestra needs to perform below the stage.
L'orchestre doit faire la performance sous la scène.
I like to listen to this type of music. I hope to hear a good song.
J'aime écouter ce type de musique. J'espère entendre une bonne chanson.
The common musical instruments that are used in a concert are drums, guitars, pianos, trumpets, violins, and flutes.
Les instruments de musique couramment utilisés dans un concert sont les tambours, les guitares, les pianos, les trompettes, les violons et les flûtes.
The art gallery has a studio for rent.
La galerie d'art a un studio à louer.
I went to an art museum yesterday.
Je suis allé hier a un musée d'art

FOOD - NOURRITURE / ALIMENTATION

Grocery store - Épicerie / **Market** - Marché / **Supermarket** - Supermarché
Groceries - Produits alimentaires / L'épicerie
Butcher shop - Boucherie / **Butcher** - Boucher
Bakery - Boulangerie / **Baker** - Boulanger / (f) Boulangière
Breakfast – Petit déjeuner / **Lunch** – Le déjeuner / **Dinner** – Dîner
Meat - Viande / **Chicken** - Poulet
Seafood – Fruit de mer
Egg – Oeuf
Milk - Lait / **Cheese** - Fromage / **Butter** – Beurre
Bread - Pain
Oil - Huile
Flour - Farine
Baked - Au four
Cake - Gâteau
Beer - Bière / **Wine** – Vin
Cinnamon - Cannelle
Powder - Poudre
Mustard - Moutarde

Where is the nearest grocery store?
Où est la plus proche épicerie?
Where can I buy meat and chicken?
Où puis-je acheter de la viande et du poulet?
I need to buy flour, eggs, milk, butter, and oil to bake my cake.
J'ai besoin d'acheter de la farine, des œufs, du lait, du beurre et d'huile pour faire mon gâteau.
The groceries are already in the car.
Les produits sont déjà dans la voiture.
Where can I buy beer and wine.
Où puis-je acheter de la bière et du vin.
On which aisle is the cinnamon powder?
Dans quelle allée se trouve la cannelle en poudre?
The butcher shop is near the bakery.
La boucherie est près de la boulangerie.
I have to go to the market, to buy a half kilo of meat.
Je dois aller au marché, pour acheter un demi-kilo de viande.
For lunch, we can eat seafood, and then pasta for dinner.
Pour le déjeuner, nous pouvons manger des fruits de mer, puis des pâtes pour le dîner.
I usually eat bread with cheese for breakfast.
Habituellement je mange du pain avec du fromage pour le petit déjeuner.
I don't have any ketchup or mustard to put on my hotdog.
Je n'ai ni ketchup ni moutarde à mettre sur mon hot-dog.

Menu - Menu
Beef - Boeuf / **Lamb -** Agneau / **Pork -** Porc
Steak - Bifteck
Hamburger - Hamburger
Water – Eau
Salad - Salade / **Soup -** Soupe
Appetizer – Apéritif / **Entrée –** Entrée
Cooked - Cuit / **Boiled -** Bouillis
Fried - Frit / **Grilled / broiled -** Grillé
Raw - Crus
Dessert – Dessert
Ice cream - Crème glacée
Coffee – Café
Olive oil – Huile d'olive
Fish – Poisson
Juice - Jus
Tea – Thé
Honey - Miel
Sugar - Sucre

Do you have a menu in English?
Avez-vous un menu en anglais?
Which is preferable, the fried fish or the grilled lamb?
Lequel est préférable, le poisson frit ou l'agneau grillé?
I want to order a cup of water, a soup for my appetizer, and pizza for my entrée.
Je veux commander une verre d'eau, une soupe pour mon apéritif et une pizza pour mon entrée.
I want to order a steak for myself, a hamburger for my son, and ice cream for my wife.
Je veux commander un bifteck pour moi, un hamburger pour mon fils et une glace pour ma femme.
Which type of dessert is included with my coffee?
Quel type de dessert est inclus avec mon café?
Can I order a salad with a hard boiled egg and olive oil on the side?
Puis-je commander une salade avec un œuf dur et de l'huile d'olive a côté?
Is the piece of fish in the sushi cooked or raw?
Le morceau de poisson dans le sushi est-il cuit ou cru?
I want to order a fruit juice instead of a soda.
Je veux commander un jus de fruit au lieu d'une soda.
I want to order tea with a teaspoon of honey instead of sugar.
Je veux commander du thé avec une cuillère à café de miel au lieu du sucre.
The tip is 20% at this restaurant.
Le pourboire est de 20% (vingt pour cent) dans ce restaurant.

Foods

Vegetarian - Végétarien / (f) végétarienne
Vegan – Végétalien / (f) végétalienne
Dairy - Laitiers / **Dairy products** - Produits laitiers
Salt - Sel
Pepper - Poivre
Flavor - Saveur
Spices - Épices
Rice - Riz
Fries - Frites
Soy - Soja
Nuts - Noix / **Peanuts** - Cacahuètes / arachides
Sauce - Sauce
Sandwich - Sandwich
Mayonnaise - Mayonnaise
Jelly - Marmelade
Chocolate - Chocolat / **Cookies** - Biscuits / **Candy** - Bonbons
Whipped cream - Crème fouettée
Popsicle - Popsicle
Frozen - Congelée / **Thawed** – Décongelé

I don't eat meat because I am a vegetarian.
Je ne mange pas de la viande parce que je suis végétarienne.
My brother won't eat dairy products because he is a vegan.
Mon frère ne mangera pas de produits laitiers parce qu'il est végétalien.
Food tastes much better with salt, pepper, and other spices.
Les aliments ont un meilleur goût avec du sel, du poivre et des épices.
The only things I have in my freezer are popsicles.
Les seules choses que j'ai dans mon congélateur sont des sucettes glacées.
No chocolate, candy, or whipped cream until after dinner.
Pas de chocolat, de bonbons ou de crème fouettée avant le dîner.
I want to try a sample of that piece of cheese.
Je veux essayer un échantillon de ce morceau de fromage.
I have allergies to nuts and peanuts.
J'ai des allergies aux noix et aux arachides.
This sauce is disgusting.
Cette sauce est dégoûtante.
Why do you always put mayonnaise on your sandwich?
Pourquoi mettez-vous toujours de la mayonnaise dans votre sandwich?
The food is still frozen so we need to wait for it to thaw.
La nourriture est toujours congelée, nous devons donc attendre qu'elle dégèle.
Please bring me a bowl of cereal and a slice of toasted bread with jelly.
Apportez-moi un bol de céréales et une tranche de pain grillé avec de la marmelade.
It's healthier to eat rice instead of fries.
Il est meilleur santé de manger du riz que des frites.

VEGETABLES - VEGETABLES

Grilled vegetables – Légumes grillés / **Steamed vegetables** – Légumes à la vapeur
Tomato - Tomate / **Carrot** - Carotte / **Lettuce** - Salade
Radish - Radis
Beet - Betterave
Eggplant - Aubergine
Bell Pepper – Poivron / **Hot pepper** – Piment
Celery - Céleri
Spinach - Épinard
Cabbage - Chou
Cauliflower - Choufleur
Beans – Haricots
Corn - Maïs
Garlic - Ail / **Onion** - Oignon
Artichoke - Artichaut

Grilled vegetables or steamed vegetables are popular side dishes at restaurants.
Les légumes grillés ou les légumes cuites à la vapeur sont des accompagnements populaires dans les restaurants.
I put carrots, bell peppers, lettuce, and radishes in my salad.
J'ai mis des carottes, des poivrons, de la laitue et des radis dans ma salade.
It's not hard to grow tomatoes.
Il n'est pas difficile de cultiver des tomates.
Eggplant can be cooked or fried.
L'aubergine peut être cuite ou frite.
I like beets in my salad.
J'aime les betteraves dans ma salade.
Why are chili peppers so spicy?
Pourquoi les piments sont-ils si picants?
Celery and spinach have natural vitamins.
Le céleri et les épinards contiennent des vitamines naturelles.
Fried cauliflower tastes better than fried cabbage.
Le chou-fleur frit a meilleur goût que le chou frit.
Rice and beans are my favorite side dish.
Le riz et les haricots sont mon plat d'accompagnement préféré.
I like to put butter on corn.
J'aime mettre du beurre sur le maïs.
Garlic is an important ingredient in many cuisines.
L'ail est un ingrédient important dans de nombreuses cuisines.
Where is the onion powder?
Où est la poudre d'oignon?
Artichokes are difficult to peel.
Les artichaux son difficile a peler.

Cucumber – Concombre
Lentils - Lentilles
Peas - Pois
Green onion – Oignon vert
Herbs - Herbes
Basil - Basilic / **Cilantro** - Coriandre
Dill - Aneth / **Parsley** - Persil / **Mint** - Menthe
Potatoe – Pomme de terre / **Sweet Potato** - Patate douce
Mushroom – Champignon
Asparagus - Asperges
Seaweed – Algue
Pumpkin – Citrouille
Squash - Courge / **Zucchini** - Zucchini / courgettes
Chick peas – Pois chiches
Vegetable garden – Potager

I want to order lentil soup.
Je veux commander une soupe aux lentilles.
Please put the green onion in the refrigerator.
Veuillez mettre l'oignon vert au réfrigérateur.
The most common kitchen herbs are basil, cilantro, dill, parsley, and mint.
Les herbes de cuisine les plus courantes sont le basilic, la coriandre, l'aneth, le persil et la menthe.
Some of the most common vegetables for tempura are sweet potatoes and mushrooms.
Les légumes les plus courants pour la tempura sont les patates douces et les champignons.
I want to order vegetarian sushi with asparagus and cucumber along with a side of seaweed salad.
Je veux commander des sushis végétariens avec des asperges et du concombre et a côté une salade d'algues.
I enjoy eating pumpkin seeds as a snack.
J'aime manger des graines de citrouille comme collation.
I must water my vegetable garden.
Je dois arroser mon potager.
The potatoes in the field are ready to harvest.
Les pommes de terre des champs sont prêtes à être récoltées.
Chickpeas are a popular ingredient in Middle Eastern food.
Les pois chiches sont un ingrédient populaire dans la nourriture du Moyen-Orient.
Is there Zucchini in the soup?
Y a-t-il des courgettes dans la soupe?
I like to put ginger dressing on my salad.
J'aime mettre de la vinaigrette au gingembre dans ma salade.
The tomatoes are fresh but the cucumbers are rotten.
Le tomates sont fraiches mais les comcombres sont pouris.

FRUITS - FRUITS

Apple - Pomme / **Banana -** Banane
Orange - Orange / **Grapefruit -** Pamplemousse
Peach - Pêche
Tropical fruit - Fruit tropical
Papaya - Papaye / **Coconut -** Noix de coco
Cherry - Cerise
Raisins - Raisins secs / **Prunes -** Pruneaux / **Dates -** Dattes
Figs - Figues
Fruit salad - Salade de fruit
Dried fruit - Fruit sec
Apricot - Abricot
Pear - Poire
Avocado - Avocat
Ripe - Mûr

Can I add raisins to the apple pie?
Puis-je ajouter des raisins secs à la tarte aux pommes?
Orange juice is a wonderful source of Vitamin C.
Le jus d'orange est une merveilleuse source de vitamine C.
Grapefruits are extremely beneficial for your health.
Les pamplemousses sont extrêmement bénéficiaire pour votre santé.
I have a peach tree in my front yard.
J'ai un arbre des pêches dans ma cour.
I bought papayas and coconuts at the supermarket to prepare a tropical fruit salad.
J'ai acheté des papayes et des noix de coco au supermarché pour préparer une salade de fruits tropicaux.
I want to travel to Japan to see the famous cherry blossom.
Je veux voyager au Japon pour voir la célèbre floraison du cerisier.
Bananas are tropical fruits.
Les bananes sont des fruits tropicaux.
I want to mix dates and figs in my fruit salad.
Je veux mélanger les dattes et les figues dans ma salade de fruits.
Apricots and prunes are my favorite dried fruits.
Les abricots et les pruneaux sont mes fruits secs preferes.
Pears are delicious.
Les poires sont délicieuses.
The avocados aren't ripe yet.
Les avocats ne sont pas encore mûrs.
The green apple is very sour.
La pomme verte est très aigre.
The unripe peach is usually bitter.
Généralement la pêche qui n'est pas mûre, est amère.

Fruit tree - Arbre fruitier
Citrus - Citrus
Lemon - Citron / **Lime -** Citron vert
Pineapple - Ananas
Melon - Melon / **Watermelon -** Pastèque
Strawberry - Fraise
Berry - Murs
Raspberry - Framboise
Blueberry - Myrtille
Grapes - Les raisins
Pomegranate - Grenade
Plum - Prune
Olive - Olive
Grove - Verger

Strawberries grow during the Spring.
Les fraises poussent au printemps.
How much does the watermelon juice cost?
Combien coûte le jus de pastèque?
I have a pineapple plant inside a pot.
J'ai une plante d'ananas dans un pot.
Melons grow on the ground.
Les melons poussent sur le sol.
I am going to the fruit-tree section of the nursery today to purchase a few citrus trees.
Je vais aujourd'hui à la section des arbres fruitiers de la pépinière pour acheter quelques citrus.
There are many raspberries growing on the bush.
Il ya des nombreuses framboises qui poussent dans la brousse.
Blueberry juice is very sweet.
Le jus de myrtille est très doux.
Berries are acidic fruits.
Les baies sont des fruits acides.
Pomegranate juice contains a very high level of antioxidants.
Le jus de grenade contient un niveau très élevé d'antioxydants.
I need to pick the grapes to make the wine.
Je dois cueillir les raisins pour faire du vin.
Plums are seasonal fruits.
Les prunes sont des fruits de saison.
I want to add either lemon juice or lime juice to my salad.
Je veux ajouter du jus de citron ou du jus de citron vert à ma salade.
I have an olive grove in my backyard.
J'ai un olivier dans mon verger.

SHOPPING - DES ACHATS

Clothes - Vêtements
Clothing store - Magasin de vêtements
For sale - À vendre
Hat - Chapeau
Shirt - Chemise
Shoes - Chaussures
Skirt - Jupe **/ Dress -** Robe
Pants - Pantalon
Shorts - Shorts
Suit - Costume
Vest - Gilet
Tie - Attacher
Uniform - Uniforme
Belt - Ceinture
Socks - Chaussettes
Gloves - Gants
Glasses - Lunettes **/ Sunglasses -** Lunettes de soleil
Size - Taille **/ Small -** Petit **/ (f)** petite **/ Medium -** Moyen **/ Large -** Grande
Thick - Épais **/ Thin -** Maigre
Thrift store - Friperie

There are a lot of clothes for sale today.
Il y a beaucoup de vêtements à vendre aujourd'hui.
Does this hat look good?
Ce chapeau a-t-il l'air bien?
I am happy with this shirt and these shoes.
Je suis content de cette chemise et de ces chaussures.
She prefers a skirt instead of a dress.
Elle préfère une jupe plutôt qu'une robe.
These pants aren't my size.
Ce pantalon n'est pas ma taille.
Where can I find a thrift store? I want to buy a suit, a vest, and a tie.
Où puis-je trouver une friperie? Je veux acheter un costume, un gilet et une cravate.
There are uniforms for school at the clothing store.
Il y a des uniformes pour l'école au magasin de vêtements.
I forgot my socks, belt, and shorts at your house.
J'ai oublié mes chaussettes, ma ceinture et mon short chez toi.
These gloves are a size too small. Do you have a medium size?
Ces gants sont d'une taille trop petite. Avez-vous une taille moyenne?
Today I don't need my reading glasses. I only need my sunglasses.
Aujourd'hui, je n'ai plus besoin de mes lunettes de lecture. Je n'ai besoin que de mes lunettes de soleil.

Jacket - Jaquette
Scarf - Écharpe
Mittens - Mouffles
Sleeve - Manche
Boots (rain, winter) - Bottes
Sweater - Pullover
Bathing suit - Maillot de bain
Flip flops - Tongs
Tank top - Débardeur
Sandals - Sandales
Heels - Talons
On sale - En soldes / en vente
Expensive - Coûteux / cher
Free - Gratuit **/ Discount -** Remise
Cheap - Pas cher
Shopping - Achats
Mall - Centre commercial

We are going to the mountain today so don't forget your jacket, mittens, and scarf.
Nous allons à la montagne aujourd'hui, alors n'oubliez pas votre veste, vos mouffles et votre écharpe.
I have long sleeve shirts and short sleeve shirts.
J'ai des chemises à manches longues et des chemises à manches courtes.
Boots and sweaters are meant for winter.
Les bottes et les pulls sont destinés à l'hiver.
At the beach, I wear a bathing suit and flip flops.
À la plage, je porte un maillot de bain et des tongs.
I want to buy a tank top for summer.
Je veux acheter un débardeur pour l'été.
I can't wear heels on the beach, only sandals.
Je ne peux pas porter des talons pour la plage, que des sandales.
What will be on sale tomorrow?
Que sera-il en vente demain?
This is free.
C'est gratuit.
Even though these colognes and perfumes are discounted, they are still very expensive.
Même si ces eaux de Cologne et parfums sont à prix réduit, ils sont encore très chers.
These items are very cheap.
Ces articles sont très bon marché.
I can go shopping only on weekends.
Je ne peux faire du shopping que le week-end.
Is the local mall far?
Le centre commercial local est-il loin?

Shopping

Store - Boutique
Business hours - Heures de travail
Open - Ouvert
Closed - Fermé
Entrance - Entrée / **Exit** - Sortie
Shopping cart / Shopping basket - Panier
Shopping bag - Sac de courses
Toy store - Magasin de jouets / **Toy** - Jouet
Book store - Librairie / **Music store** - Magasin de musique
Jeweler - Bijoutier, **(f)** bijoutière / **Jewelry** - Bijoux
Gold - Or / **Silver** - Argent / **Diamond** - Diamant
Necklace - Collier / **Bracelet** - Bracelet / **Earrings** - Boucles d'oreilles
Gift - Cadeau
Coin - Pièce de monnaie
Antique - Antique
Dealer - Marchand / (f) marchande

What are your (plural) business hours?
Quelles sont vos heures d'ouverture?
What time does the store open?
À quelle heure le magasin ouvre-t-il?
What time does the store close?
À quelle heure le magasin ferme-t-il?
Where is the entrance?
Où est l'entrée?
Where is the exit?
Où est la sortie?
My children want to go to the toy store so they can fill up the shopping cart with toys.
Mes enfants veulent aller au magasin de jouets pour pouvoir remplir le panier de jouets.
I need a large shopping basket when I go to the supermarket.
J'ai besoin d'un grand panier lorsque je vais au supermarché.
There is a sale at the bookstore right now.
Il ya une solde dans le librarie maintenant.
It's difficult to find a music store these days.
Il est difficile de trouver un magasin de musique de ces jours.
The jeweler sells gold and silver.
Le bijoutier vend de l'or et de l'argent.
I want to buy a diamond necklace.
Je veux acheter un collier en diamant.
This bracelet and those pair of earrings are gifts for my daughter.
Ce bracelet et ces boucles d'oreilles sont des cadeaux pour ma fille.
He is an antique coin dealer.
Il est antiquaire de pièce de monnaie.

FAMILY - FAMILLE

Mother - Mère
Father - Père
Son - Fils
Daughter - Fille
Brother - Frère
Sister - Sœur
Husband - Mari
Wife - Épouse / femme
Parents - Parents
Child - Enfant
Baby - Bébé
Grandparents - Grands-parents
Grandfather - Grand-père
Grandmother - Grand-mère
Grandson - Petit fils
Granddaughter - Petite fille
Grandchildren - Petits enfants
Nephew - Neveu **/ Niece -** Nièce
Cousin - (M) Cousin / **(F)** Cousine

I have a big family.
J'ai une grande famille.
My brother and sister are here.
Mon frère et ma sœur sont ici.
The mother and father want to spend time with their child.
La mère et le père veulent passer du temps avec leur enfant.
He wants to bring his son and daughter.
Il veut amener son fils et sa fille.
The grandfather wants to take his grandson to the movie.
Le grand-père veut emmener son petit-fils au cinema.
The grandmother needs to give her granddaughter money.
La grand-mère doit donner de l'argent à sa petite-fille.
The grandparents want to spend time with their grandchildren.
Les grands-parents veulent passer du temps avec leurs petits-enfants.
The husband and wife have a new baby.
Le mari et la femme ont un nouveau bébé.
I want to go to the park with my niece and nephew.
Je veux aller au parc avec ma nièce et mon neveu.
My cousin wants to see his children.
Mon cousin veut voir ses enfants.
That man is a good parent.
Cet homme est un bon parent.

Aunt - Tante
Uncle - Oncle
Man - Homme / **Woman** - Femme
Stepfather - Parâtre / **Stepmother** - Marâtre
Stepson - Beau-fils / **Stepdaughter** - Belle fille
Stepbrother - Beau-frère / **Stepsister** - Belle-soeur
Half brother - Demi-frère / **Half sister** - Demi-sœur
Ancestor - Ancêtre / **Family tree** - Arbre généalogique
Generation - Génération
Relative - Proche famille / **Family member** - Membre de famille
First born - Premier né
Only child - Fils unique
Twins - Jumeaux / (f) jumelles
Pregnant - En ceinte
Adopted child - Enfant adopté
Orphan - Orphelin / (f) orpheline
Adult - Adulte
Neighbor - Voisin, **(f)** voisine/ **Friend** - Ami, (f) amie /**Roommate** - Colocataire

My aunt and uncle came to visit.
Ma tante et mon oncle sont venus visiter.
He is their only child.
Il est leur unique enfant.
My wife is pregnant with twins.
Ma femme est enceinte avec des jumeaux.
He is their eldest son.
Il est leur fils aîné.
The first-born child usually takes on all the responsibilities.
Le premier-né assume généralement toutes les responsabilités.
I was able to find all my relatives and ancestors on my family tree.
J'ai pu trouver tous mes ancêtres et proche membres de famille dans mon arbre généalogique.
My parents' generation loved disco music.
La génération de mes parents aimait la musique disco.
Their adopted child was an orphan.
Leur enfant adopté était un orphelin.
I have a nice neighbor.
J'ai un gentile voisin / voisine.
We need to choose a godfather for the baby.
Nous devons choisir un parrain pour le bebe.
She considers her stepson as her real son.
Elle considère son beau-fils comme son vrai fils.
She is his stepdaughter.
Elle est sa belle-fille.

HUMAN BODY - LE CORP HUMAIN

Head - Tête
Face - Visage
Eye - Œil
Ear - Oreille
Nose - Nez
Mouth - Bouche / **Lips -** Lèvres
Tongue - Langue
Cheek - Joue
Chin - Menton
Neck - Cou / **Throat -** Gorge
Forehead - Front
Eyebrow - Sourcil / **Eyelashes -** Cils
Hair - Cheveux / **Beard -** Barbe / **Mustache -** Moustache
Tooth - Dent

My chin, cheeks, mouth, lips, and eyes are all part of my face.
Mon menton, mes joues, ma bouche, mes lèvres et mes yeux font tous partie de mon visage.
He has small ears.
Il a de petites oreilles.
I have a cold so my nose, eyes, mouth, and tongue are affected.
J'ai un rhume, donc mon nez, mes yeux, ma bouche et ma langue sont affectés.
The five senses are sight, touch, taste, smell, and hearing.
Les cinq sens sont la vue, le toucher, le goût, l'odorat et l'ouïe.
I am washing my face right now.
En ce moment je lave mon visage.
I have a headache.
J'ai mal à la tête.
My eyebrows are too long.
Mes sourcils sont trop longs.
He must shave his beard and mustache.
Il doit se raser la barbe et les moustaches.
I brush my teeth every morning.
Je me brosse les dents tous les matins.
She puts makeup on her cheeks and lipstick on her lips.
Elle met du maquillage sur ses joues et du rouge à lèvres sur ses lèvres.
Her hair covered her forehead.
Ses cheveux couvrent son front.
She has a long neck.
Elle a un long cou.
I have a sore throat.
J'ai mal à la gorge.

Shoulder - Épaule
Chest - Poitrine
Arm - Bras / **Elbow** - Coude / **Wrist** - Poignet
Hand - Main / **Palm** (of hand) - Paume
Finger - Doigt
Thumb - Pouce
Back - Retour
Belly - Ventre / **Stomach** - Estomac / **Intestines** - Intestins
Brain - Cerveau / **Heart** - Cœur / **Kidneys** - Reins / **Lungs** - Poumons / **Liver** - Foie
Leg - Jambe / **Ankle** - La cheville / **Foot** - Pied
Toe - Doigt du pied
Nail - Ongle
Joint - Articulation
Muscle - Muscle
Skeleton - Squelette / **Bone** - Os, (p) Osses
Spine - Colonne vertébrale / **Ribs** - Côtes / **Skull** - Crâne
Skin - Peau
Vein - Veine

He has a problem with his stomach.
Il a un problème d'estomac.
The brain, heart, kidneys, lungs, and liver are internal organs.
Le cerveau, le cœur, les reins, les poumons et le foie sont des organes internes.
His chest and shoulders are very muscular.
Sa poitrine et ses épaules sont très musclées.
I need to strengthen my arms and legs.
J'ai besoin de renforcer mes bras et mes jambes.
I accidentally hit his wrist with my elbow.
J'ai accidentellement frappé son poignet avec mon coude.
I have pain in every part of my body especially in my hand, ankle, and back.
J'ai des douleurs dans toutes les parties de mon corps, en particulier dans ma main, ma cheville et mon dos.
I want to cut my nails.
Je veux me couper les ongles.
I need a new bandage for my thumb.
J'ai besoin d'un nouveau bandage pour mon pouce.
I have a cast on my foot because of a broken bone.
J'ai un plâtre au pied à cause d'une fracture osseuse.
I have muscles and joint pain today.
Aujourd'hui j'ai des douleurs des muscles et articulaires.
The spine is the main part of the body.
La colonne vertébrale est la partie principale du corps.
I have beautiful skin.
J'ai une belle peau.

HEALTH AND MEDICAL - SANTÉ ET MÉDICAL

Disease - Maladie
Bacteria - Les bactéries
Sick - Malade
Clinic - Clinique
Headache - Mal de tête
Earache - Mal d'oreille
Pharmacy - Pharmacie / **Prescription** - Ordonnance
Symptoms - Symptômes
Nausea - La nausée / **Stomachache** - Mal d'estomac
Allergy - Allergie
Penicillin - Pénicilline / **Antibiotic** - Antibiotique
Sore throat - Gorge irritée
Fever - Fièvre / **Flu** - Grippe
Cough - La toux / **To cough** - Tousser
Infection - Infection
Injury - Blessure / **Scar** - Cicatrice
Ache - Mal, (p) maux / **Pain** - Douleur
Intensive care - Soins intensifs
Bandaid - Pansement / **Bandage** - Bandage

Are you in good health?
Etes vous en bonne santé?
These bacteria caused this disease.
Ces bactéries ont causé cette maladie.
He is very sick.
Il est très malade.
I have a headache so I must go to the pharmacy to refill my prescription.
J'ai mal à la tête, je dois donc aller à la pharmacie pour renouveler mon ordonnance.
The main symptoms of food poisoning are nausea and stomach ache.
Les symptômes principaux d'intoxication alimentaire sont les nausées et les mal d'estomac.
I have an allergy to penicillin, so I need another antibiotic.
Je suis allergique à la pénicilline, j'ai donc besoin d'un autre antibiotique.
What do I need to treat an earache?
De quoi ai-je besoin pour traiter un mal d'oreille?
I need to go to the clinic for my fever and sore throat.
Je dois y aller à la clinique pour ma fièvre et mon mal de gorge.
The bandage won't help your infection.
Le bandage n'aidera pas votre infection.
I have a serious injury so I must go to intensive care.
J'ai une grave blessure, donc je dois aller aux soins intensifs.
I have muscle and joint pains today.
J'ai des douleurs musculaires et articulaires aujourd'hui.

Hospital - Hôpital
Doctor - Médecin / **Nurse** - Infirmier, (f) infirmière
Family Doctor - Médecin de famille / **Pediatrician** - Pédiatre
Medication - Des médicaments / **Pills** - Pilules
Heartburn - Brûlures d'estomac
Paramedic - Paramédical / (f) paramédicale
Emergency room - Salle d'urgence
Health insurance - Assurance de santé
Patient - Patient / (f) patiente
Surgery - Chirurgie / **Surgeon** - Chirurgien
Anesthesia - Anesthésie
Local anesthesia - Anesthésie locale / **General anesthesia** - Anesthésie générale
Wheelchair - Fauteuil roulant / **A walker** - Un promeneur / **A cane** - Une canne
Stretcher - Civière / tendeur
Dialysis - Dialyse / **Insulin** - Insuline / **Diabetes** - Diabète
Temperature - Température / **Thermometer** - Thermomètre
A shot - La piqûre / **Needle** - Aiguille / **Syringe** - Seringue

Where is the closest hospital?
Où est l'hôpital le plus proche?
Usually we see the nurse before the doctor.
Habituellement, nous voyons l'infirmière avant le médecin.
The paramedics can take her to the emergency room but she doesn't have health insurance.
Les ambulanciers peuvent l'emmener aux urgences mais elle n'a pas d'assurance.
The doctor treated the patient.
Le médecin a soigné le patient.
He needs knee surgery today.
Il a besoin d'une opération au genou aujourd'hui.
The surgeon needs to administer general anesthesia in order to operate on the patient.
Le chirurgien doit administrer une anesthésie générale afin d'opérer le patient.
Does the patient need a wheelchair or a stretcher?
Le patient a-t-il besoin d'un fauteuil roulant ou d'une civière?
I have to take medicine every day.
Je dois prendre des médicaments tous les jours.
Do you have any pills for heartburn?
Avez-vous des pilules pour les brûlures d'estomac?
Where is the closest dialysis center?
Où est le centre de dialyse le plus proche?
The doctor didn't prescribe insulin for my diabetes.
Le médecin n'a pas prescrit d'insuline pour ma diabète.
I need a thermometer to take my temperature.
J'ai besoin d'un thermomètre pour prendre ma température.

Health

Stroke - Accident vasculaire cérébral
Blood - Du sang / **Blood pressure** - Pression artérielle
Heart attack - Attaque cardiaque
Cancer - Cancer / **Chemotherapy** - Chimiothérapie
To help - Aider
Germs - Germes / **Virus** - Virus
Vaccine - Vaccin / **A cure** - Un remède / **To cure** - Guérir
Nutrition - Nutrition / **Diet** - Régime / **Cholesterol** - Cholestérol
Blind - Aveugle / **Deaf** - Sourd / **Mute** - Muet
Young - Jeune / **Elderly** - Personnes âgées
Fat - Gras / **Fat** (person) - Gros, **(f)** Grosse / **Skinny** (person) - Maigre
Nursing home - Maison de retraite
Disability - Invalidité / **Handicap** - Handicap, invalidité / **Paralysis** - Paralysie
Depression - La dépression / **Anxiety** - Anxiété
Dentist - Dentiste
X-ray - Radiographie
Tooth cavity - Cavité dentaire
Tooth paste - Pâte dentifrice / **Tooth brush** - Brosse à dents

A stroke is caused by a lack of blood flow to the brain.
Un accident vasculaire cérébral est causé par un manque de circulation sanguine vers le cerveau.
These are the symptoms of a heart attack.
Ce sont les symptômes d'une crise cardiaque.
Chemotherapy is for treating cancer.
La chimiothérapie sert à traiter le cancer.
Proper nutrition is very important and you must avoid foods that are high in cholesterol.
Une bonne nutrition est très importante et vous devez éviter les aliments riches en cholestérol.
I am starting my diet today.
Je commence mon régime aujourd'hui.
There is no cure for this virus, only a vaccine.
Il n'y a pas de remède pour ce virus, seulement une vaccine.
The nursing home is open 365 days a year.
La maison de retraite est ouverte 365 jours par an.
I don't like suffering from depression and anxiety.
Je n'aime pas souffrir de dépression et d'anxiété.
Soap and water kill germs.
Le savon et l'eau tuent les germes.
The dentist took X-rays of my teeth to check for cavities.
Le dentiste a pris des radiographies de mes dents pour vérifier les caries.
In the morning I put tooth paste on my toothrbush
Ce matin, j'ai mis la pâté dentifrice sur ma brosse à dents.

EMERGENCY & DISASTERS - URGENCE ET CATASTROPHE

Emergency - Urgence
Help - Sauve-moi!
Fire - Feu
Ambulance - Ambulance
First aid - Premiers secours
CPR - CPR (réanimation cardio-respiratoire)
Emergency number - Numéro d'urgence
Accident - Accident
Car crash - Accident de voiture
Death - Décès **/ Deadly -** Mortel **/ Fatality -** Fatalité
Lightly wounded - Légèrement blessé
Moderately wounded - Modérément blessé
Seriously wounded - Gravement blessé
Fire truck - Camion de pompier **/ Siren -** Sirène
Fire extinguisher - Extincteur d'incendie
Police - Police **/ Police station -** Poste de police
Robbery - Vol / brigandage
Thief - Voleur

There is a fire. I need to call for help.
Il y a un incendi. J'ai besoin d'appeler une aide.
I need to call an ambulance.
J'ai besoin d'appeler une ambulance.
That accident was bad.
Cet accident était grave.
The car crash was fatal, there were two deaths, and four suffered serious injuries.
L'accident de voiture a été mortel, il y a eu deux morts et quatre gravement blessés.
One was moderately wounded and two were lightly wounded.
L'un était modérément blessé et deux légèrement blessés.
CPR is a first step of first-aid.
La RCR est une première étape des soins premiers.
Please provide me with the emergency number.
Veuillez me fournir le numéro d'urgence.
The police are on their way.
La police est en route.
I must call the police station to report a robbery.
Je dois appeler le poste de police pour signaler un vol.
The siren of the fire truck is very loud.
La sirène du camion de pompiers est très forte.
Where is the fire extinguisher?
Où est l'extincteur?

Fire hydrant - Bouche d'incendie
Fireman - Pompier / (f) Pompière
Emergency situation - Situation d'urgence
Explosion - Explosion
Rescue - Porter secours
Natural disaster - Catastrophe naturelle
Destruction - Destruction
Damage - Dommage / dégâts
Hurricane - Ouragan
Refuge - Refuge
Caused - Causé
Tornado - Tornade
Flood - Inondation
Storm - Orage
Snowstorm - Tempête de neige
Hail - Grêle
Safety - Sécurité
Drought - Sécheresse
Famine - Famine
Poverty - La pauvreté
Epidemic - Épidémie
Pandemic - Pandémie

It's prohibited to park by the fire hydrant in case of a fire.
Il est interdit de se garer près de la bouche d'incendie en cas d'incendie.
When there is a fire, the first to arrive on scene are the firemen.
Lorsqu'il y a un incendie, les premiers à arriver sur les lieux sont les pompiers.
There is a fire. I must call for help.
Il y a un feu. Je dois appeler à l'aide.
In an emergency situation everyone needs to be rescued.
Dans une situation d'urgence, tout le monde doit être secouru.
The gas explosion led to a natural disaster.
L'explosion de gaz a provoqué une catastrophe naturelle.
The hurricane caused a lot of damage and destruction in its path.
L'ouragan a causé beaucoup de dégâts et de destruction sur son passage.
The tornado destroyed the town.
La tornade a détruit la ville.
The drought led to famine and a lot of poverty.
La sécheresse a provoqué la famine et beaucoup de pauvreté.
There were three days of flooding following the storm.
Il y a eu trois jours d'inondation après la tempête.
This is a snowstorm and not a hail storm.
Il s'agit d'une tempête de neige et non d'une tempête de grêle.

Emergency & Disasters

Dangerous - Dangereux
Danger - Danger
Warning - Avertissement
Earthquake - Tremblement de terre
Disaster - Catastrophe
Disaster area - Zone sinistrée
Evacuation - Évacuation
Mandatory - Obligatoire
Safe place - Endroit sûr
Blackout - Coupure électrique
Rainstorm - Pluie torrentielle
Lightning - Éclair
Thunder - Tonnerre
Avalanche - Avalanche
Heatwave - Vague de chaleur
Rip current - Courant de déchirure
Tsunami - Tsunami
Whirlpool - Tourbillon

We need to evacuate the buildings during the earthquake.
Nous devons evacuer les immubles pendant le tremblement de terre.
Heatwaves are usually in the summer.
Les vagues de chaleur se produisent généralement en été.
This is a disaster area, therefore there is a mandatory evacuation order.
Il s'agit d'une zone sinistrée, il existe donc un ordre d'évacuation obligatoire.
Due to the rainstorm there was a blackout for three hours.
En raison de la tempête de pluie il y a eu une panne d'électricité pendant trois heures.
Be careful during the snowstorm, because there might be an avalanche.
Soyez prudent pendant la tempête de neige, car il pourrait y avoir une avalanche.
There is a tsunami warning today.
Il y a un avertissement de tsunami aujourd'hui.
You can't swim against a rip current.
Vous ne pouvez pas nager à contre-courant.
There is a dangerous whirlpool in the ocean.
Il y a un tourbillon dangereux dans l'océan.
There is a risk of lightning today.
Il y a un risque de foudre aujourd'hui.

HOME - MAISON

Living room - Le salon
Couch - Canapé
Sofa - Canapé
Door - Porte
Closet - Placard / armoire
Stairway - Escalier
Rug - Tapis
Curtain - Rideau
Window - Fenêtre
Floor - Sol
Floor (as in level) **-** Etage
Fireplace - Foyer
Chimney - Cheminée

The living room is missing a couch.
Le salon manque un canapé.
I must buy a new door for my closet.
Je dois acheter une nouvelle porte pour mon placard.
The spiral staircase is beautiful.
L'escalier en colimaçon est magnifique.
There aren't any curtains on the windows.
Il n'y a pas de rideaux sur les fenêtres.
I have a marble floor on the first floor and a wooden floor on the second floor.
J'ai un sol en marbre au premier étage et un plancher en bois au deuxième étage.
The fire sparkles in the fireplace.
Le feu scintille dans la foyer.
I can clean the floors today and then I want to arrange the closet.
Je peux nettoyer les sols aujourd'hui et ensuite je veux ranger le placard.
I have to wash the rug with laundry detergent.
Je dois laver le tapis avec un détergent à lessive.

Home

Silverware - Argenterie
Knife - Couteau / **Spoon** - Cuillère / **Fork** - Fourchette / **Teaspoon** - Cuillère à café
Kitchen - Cuisine
A cup - Une tasse
Plate - Assiette
Bowl - Bol
Napkin - Serviette de table
Table - Table
Placemat - Set de table
Table cloth - Nappe de table
Glass (material) - Verre
A glass (cup) - Un verre
Oven - Four / **Stove** - Le rèchaud
Pot (cooking) - Casserole
Pan - La poêle
Shelve - ètagère
Cabinet - Cabinet
Pantry - Garde-manger
Drawer - Tiroir

The knives, spoons, teaspoons, and forks are inside the drawer in the kitchen.
Les couteaux, cuillères, cuillères à café et fourchettes sont à l'intérieur du tiroir dans la cuisine.
There aren't enough cups, plates, and silverware on the table for everyone.
Il n'y a pas assez de tasses, d'assiettes et d'argenterie sur la table pour tout le monde.
The napkin is underneath the bowl.
La serviette est sous le bol.
The placemats are on the table.
Les napperons sont sur la table.
The table cloth is beautiful.
La nappe est jolie.
There is canned food in the pantry.
Il y a des conserves dans le garde-manger.
Where are the toothpicks?
Où sont les cure-dents?
The glasses on the shelve are used for champagne, not wine.
Les verres sur l'étagère sont utilisés pour le champagne, pas le vin.
The pizza is in the oven.
La pizza est au four.
The pots and pans are in the cabinet.
Les casseroles et poêles sont dans l'armoire.
The stove isn't functioning.
Le rèchaud ne fonctionne pas.

Bedroom - Chambre a coucher
Bed - Lit / **Blanket -** Couverture / **Bed sheet -** Drap de lit
Mattress - Matelas / **Pillow -** Oreiller
Mirror - Miroir
Chair - Chaise
Dinning room - Salle à manger
Hallway - Couloir
Downstairs - En bas
Towel - Serviette
Bathtub - Baignoire / **Shower -** Douche
Soap - Savon
Bathroom - Salle de bains / **Sink -** Évier
Bag - Sac / **Box -** Boîte
Keys - Clés
Candle - Bougie
Laundry - Lessive

The master bedroom is at the end of the hallway, and the dining room is downstairs.
La chambre principale est au bout du couloir et la salle à manger est en bas.
The mirror looks good in the bedroom.
Le miroir a l'air bien dans la chambre a coucher.
I have to buy a new bed and a new mattress.
Je dois acheter un nouveau lit et un nouveau matelas.
Where are the blankets and bed sheets?
Où sont les couvertures et les draps?
My pillows are on the chair.
Mes oreillers sont sur la chaise.
These towels are for drying your hand.
Ces serviettes sont pour sécher votre main.
The bathtub, shower, and the sink are old.
La baignoire, la douche et le lavabo sont vieux.
I need soap to wash my hands.
J'ai besoin de savon pour me laver les mains.
The guest bathroom is in the corner of the hallway.
La salle de bain d'hôtes est dans le coin du couloir.
How many boxes does he have?
Combien de boîtes a-t-il?
I can only light this candle now.
Je ne peux qu'allumer cette bougie maintenant.
I want to put my things in the plastic bag.
Je veux mettre mes affaires dans le sac en plastique.
I need to bring my keys.
Je dois apporter mes clés.

Home

Room - Pièce
Balcony - Balcon
Roof - Toit
Ceiling - Plafond
Wall - Mur
Carpet - Tapis
Attic - Grenier
Basement - Sous-sol
Trash - Ordure
Garbage can - Poubelle
Driveway - Allée
Garden - Jardin
Backyard - Arrière-cour
Jar - Pot
Doormat - Paillasson

I can install new windows for my balcony.
Je peux installer des nouvelles fenêtres pour mon balcon.
I must install a new roof.
Je dois installer un nouveau toit.
The color of my ceiling is white.
La couleur de mon plafond est blanche.
I must paint the walls.
Je dois peindre les murs.
The attic is an extra room in the house.
Le grenier est une pièce supplémentaire de la maison.
The kids are playing either in the basement or the backyard.
Les enfants jouent au sous-sol ou dans la cour.
All the glass jars are outside on the doormat.
Tous les pots en verre sont à l'extérieur sur le paillasson.
The garbage can is blocking the driveway.
La poubelle bloque l'allée.

Basic Grammatical Requirements of the French Language

* Adjectives

In English, adjectives precede the noun, but in French, it's usually the opposite. Fast car will be *voiture rapide*, cold winter will be *hiver froid*.

French adjectives are modified by the number and gender of the nouns which they are pertaining to. Every adjective can have four forms.

- * To use with a masculine noun, you leave it the way it is.
- * To use with a feminine noun, just add an e at the end.
- * To make it plural masculine, add an *s* at the end.
- * To make it plural feminine, then simply add *es* at the end.

For example: smart, intelligent; he is smart will be *il est intelligent*, she is smart *elle est intelligente*, plural masculine, *ils sont intelligents* / plural feminine, *ils sont intelligentes*.

But if the adjective ends with an *s* or *x*, then for masculine plural, add nothing, but for feminine, you must replace the *x* at the end with *se*, and for feminine plural, you replace it with *ses*.

- * "he is happy" / *il est heureux*
- * "she is happy" / *elle est heureuse*
- * "the boys are happy" / *les garçons sont heureux*
- * "the girls are happy" / *les filles sont heureuses*

Comparisons

In order to use comparisons, add *plus* and *que*. For example:

- * "darker than" / *plus sombre que*
- * "stronger than" / *plus forte que*

Time

When referring to time, *il est une heure* means "it's one o'clock."
Any number greater than one, the *heure* becomes pluralized:

- * *il est cinq heures* / "it's five o'clock"
- * *il est six heures* / "it's six o'clock"

Basic Grammatical Requirements of French

Verbs

French verbs are conjugated in a different form than English verbs. To make a verb negative, add *ne* before the verb and *pas* after. For example:

- * I don't want / *je ne veux pas*

- I don't see / *je ne vois pas*
- I can't / *je ne peux pas*
- I don't like / *je n'aime pas*

Since *aime* ("like") begins with a vowel, the *e* in *ne* is eliminated, and it connects to the verb with an apostrophe.

*a contraction is used when the word which follows *ne* begins with a vowel)

Demonstratives

"This" (*ceci*) and "that" (*cela*) are the formal ways of reference to "this" and "that." But instead, use *ce* and *ça*, which are the spoken form. Both *ce* (*cette*, feminine tense of *ce*, and *ces* is the plural of *ce* and *cette*) and *ça* could mean the same thing: "this," "that," and "it." The difference between the two is that *ce* usually goes with a noun, neutral, or the verb *être* ("to be").

Noun:
- "that place" / *ce lieu*
- "that house" / *cette maison*
- "these days" / *ces jours*

Verb *être* ("to be"):
- "that is a boy" / *c'est un garçon*
- "that is very easy" / *c'est très facile*
- "it is not impossible" / *ce n'est pas impossible*

Since "is" is a form of the verb "to be," "that is" or "this is" (both words connect) *ce +est =c'est*, 'it's not" or 'this/that is not" is *ce n'est*.

Neutral:
- "this idea" / *cette idée*
- "that journey" / *ce voyage*

"Idea" and "journey" are neutral since they can be either male or female.

Ça usually goes with any other verb besides *être*:
- "I want this" / *je veux ça*
- "I don't need this" / *je n'ai pas besoin de ça*

* Both *ce* and *ça* can also be used before the verbs *pouvoir* and *devoir*:
- "this can be hard" / *ce peut être difficile*
- "this must happen" / *ce doit faire*
- "this can be hard" / *ça peut être difficile*
- "this must happen" / *ça doit faire*

Reading and Pronunciation in the French Language

French pronunciation is rather different than English, because there are multiple ways in which letters can become silent. But if you follow these following steps, it will help you in French pronunciation.

In general, most consonants in English and French sound the same.

Ge and *gi* is pronounced as "je."

H is silent.

Qu is pronounced as "k."

Ch is pronounced as "shhhhh."

Th is pronounced as "t," rather than being pronounced as "th."

Ç and the *r* in the French language are letters that don't exist in English. The *ç* sounds like an *s*. The French *r*, on the other hand, is pronounced at the back of your throat, unlike the *r* in English and Spanish.

Pronouncing Vowels in French

E sounds like "e" in "bed."
É sounds like "ay" as in "day."
Ê, È sounds like "e" in "net."
I, Y sounds like "ee."

Diphthongs

Ail sounds like "i" in "night."
An, *en*, and *em* are pronounced with a long nasal sound.
Oi sounds like "wa."
Oui sounds like "wee."
O, *au*, and *eau* sound like the "o" in float."
Ou sounds like "oo" in "pool."
U is pronounced by rounding the mouth like an "o" and saying the letter "e."

Silent Letters

The French language has silent letters that can be divided into three categories:
* E muet / elision
* H muet and aspiré
* Final consonants

In French, with words that end with an "e," the "e" is usually not pronounced, but the consonant that precedes it is. For example, *belle* is pronounced as "bell," *porte* is pronounced as "port." The letter "h" is never pronounced and is silent.

Basic Grammatical Requirements of the French Language

The Elision Rule applies to words ending in *ce, je, me, te, se, de, ne, que*, in which the last letter is omitted, as long as the following word begins with a consonant, and both connect creating one syllable:

* "I love you" / je t'aime
* "I have" / j'ai
* "I don't have" / je n'ai pas

In French, the final consonant is dropped unless there is a "c," "f," or "l," all of which are generally pronounced. For example, *bijoux* is pronounced as *bijou*, *tous* is pronounced as *tou*, *veux* is pronounced as *veu*. In the event a noun or adjective is pluralized, the "s" will be dropped as well. For example, "cat" *chat* is pronounced as *cha*, but the plural *chats* is pronounced as *chat*. Another example: *"Dans,"* meaning "in," is pronounced as *dan* (the "n" should not be stressed too strongly). There are a few exceptions though, including *avec, club, hiver, avril*, and a few others as well.

The Liaison Rule is a situation in which a consonant at the end of a word that would usually not be pronounced is pronounced because it's followed by a word that begins with a vowel or silent "h." In that situation, the "s" or "x" are pronounced as "z." "The friends," *les amis*, is pronounced as *lez-amis*. *Deux amis* is pronounced as *deuz-amis*.

Conclusion

You have now learned a wide range of sentences in relation to a variety of topics such as the home and garden. You can discuss the roof and ceiling of a house, plus natural disasters like hurricanes and thunderstorms.

The combination of sentences can also work well when caught in a natural disaster and having to deal with emergency issues. When the electricity gets cut you can tell your family or friends, "I can only light this candle now." As you're running out of the house, remind yourself of the essentials by saying, "I need to bring my keys with me."

If you need to go to a hospital, you have now been provided with sentences and the vocabulary for talking to doctors and nurses and dealing with surgery and health issues. Most importantly, you can ask, "What is the emergency number in this country?" When you get to the hospital, tell the health services, "The hurricane caused a lot of destruction and damage in its path," and "We used the hurricane shelter for refuge."

The three hundred and fifty words that you learned in part 1 should have been a big help to you with these new themes. When learning the French language, you are now more able to engage with people in French, which should make your travels flow a lot easier.

Part 3 will introduce you to additional topics that will be invaluable to your journeys. You will learn vocabulary in relation to politics, the military, and the family. The three books in this series all together provide a flawless system of learning the French language. When you visit France you will now have the capacity for greater conversational learning.

When you proceed to Part 3 you will be able to expand your vocabulary and conversational skills even further. Your range of topics will expand to the office environment, business negotiations and even school.

Please, feel free to post a review in order to share your experience or suggest feedback as to how this method can be improved.

NOTE FROM THE AUTHOR

Thank you for your interest in my work. I encourage you to share your overall experience of this book by posting a review. Your review can make a difference! Please feel free to describe how you benefited from my method or provide creative feedback on how I can improve this program. I am constantly seeking ways to enhance the quality of this product, based on personal testimonials and suggestions from individuals like you. In order to post a review, please check with the retailer of this book.

Thanks and best of luck,

Yatir Nitzany